THROUGH THE
WITH
The FAMILY CIRCUS

BY
BIL KEANE

Sell your books at
sellbackyourBook.com!
Go to sellbackyourBook.com
and get an instant price
quote. We even pay the
shipping - see what your old
books are worth today!

Inspected By: yulieth_rodriguez

00074923 87

Fawcett Columbine · New York

Sale of this book without a front cover may be unauthorized. If this
book is coverless, it may have been reported to the publisher as
"unsold or destroyed" and neither the author nor the publisher
may have received payment for it.

A Fawcett Columbine Book

Published by Ballantine Books

Copyright © 1992 by Bil Keane, Inc.
"The Family Circus" distributed by King Features Syndicate, Inc.

All rights reserved under International and Pan-American
Copyright Conventions. Published in the United States by
Ballantine Books, a division of Random House, Inc., New York,
and simultaneously in Canada by Random House of Canada
Limited, Toronto.

Library of Congress Catalog Card Number: 91-90643

ISBN 0-449-90663-9

Manufactured in the United States of America

First Edition: August 1992

10 9 8 7 6 5 4 3 2 1

Question: Which day, not including your birthday and Christmas, is your favorite day of the year?

BILLY: "The day I like best is whatever the date is in June that's the first day of summer vacation. I like to get up early and walk around outside in my bare feet and know I'm not going to hear that school bus come up the street. And the days are so long we don't have to go to bed until real late. I might even get to watch Johnny Carson."

JEFFY: "I don't remember 'cause I've only been here for three years. Dolly keeps tellin' me to say HER birthday, but that wouldn't be right. Could you ask me again when I get to be old—like 5 or 7?"

DOLLY: "Well, ummm...I was gonna say my birthday, then I thought of Christmas, but we're not allowed to say those days so I hafta think of another one, but I can't. Oh! I thought of one! JEFFY'S birthday! We all go out for hamburgers or pizza and at home I get to have lots of ice cream and cake I helped Mommy bake. And I can play with Jeffy's presents because he's only three."

PJ: (Daddy answering for 18-month-old PJ): "Well, ladies and gentlemen, out of the 363 days from which I can choose, it is extremely difficult to decide. However, my friends, I do believe it is a tossup between Mother's Day and Father's Day, and Grandparents' Day. But, then EVERY day is a favorite of mine in this great country of ours." (Daddy is considering running for the local school board).

BILLY ADDS A HOLY CHAPTER TO HIS POPULAR INSTRUCTIONAL MANUAL FOR CHILDREN EVERYWHERE.

How to Be a Good Kid In Church
By Billy (age 7)

You are in God's house. Ask to see his bathroom.

Understand thy neighbor. Stare at the people behind you and try to understand them.

Never Fall asleep in Church. Stay awake by squirming and wiggling a lot.

It's not nice to speak when there is singing or praying. Wait till there is silence, then talk loud so you can be heard.

Honor thy Father. Tell everybody how much he put in the collection basket.

Goodness is always rewarded. Tell your mom you're being good and want the candy that's in her purse.

Learn all you can about religion. Ask why the seats are called "pews."

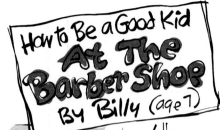

How to Be a Good Kid At The Barber Shop
By Billy (age 7)

The best way to get waited on soon is to come in **crying**!

Show your mom you love her. When she's leaving you there, attach yourself to her leg.

If some dumb ballgame or the News is on TV turn it to Cartoons. Everybody likes them.

Ask for a lollipop and keep the barber's floor clean by catching all the hair on the lollipop. Ask for another lollipop.

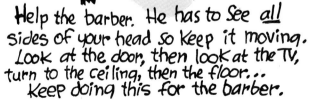

Help the barber. He has to see <u>all</u> sides of your head so keep it moving. Look at the door, then look at the TV, turn to the ceiling, then the floor... keep doing this for the barber.

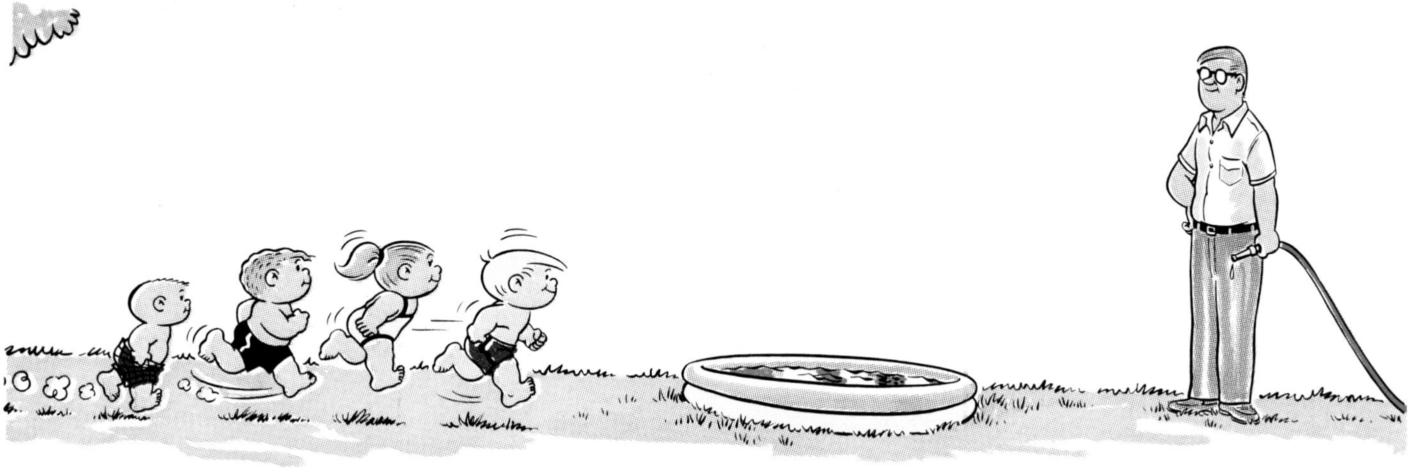

WEIGHT LIFTING

100 METER RACE

When I Grow Up I Want to Be...

...A baseball player if I can only get to First base.

...An architect, unless I have other plans.

...A parachute jumper if things open up for me.

...A banker, unless I lose interest.

...A poultry farmer if I don't chicken out.

...A mountain climber if I don't fall down on the job.

...A Golf pro if I can just stay on course.

...A TV Star if I fit into the picture.

...An Astronaut if I'm launched in the right direction.

Another page in Billy's manual for good kids everywhere.

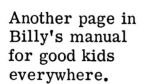

How to Be a Good Kid AT Grandma's by Me (Billy - age 7)

Help poor Grandma by telling her the **right** way to do things-- like your Mommy does them.

Show Grandma that you love her place by looking into everything! Start with the refrigerator.

Decorate her rooms by making drawings for her until all her walls are filled.

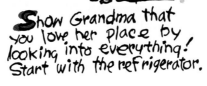

She gets tired of watching daytime serials. Put on cartoons for her.

Keep her from feeling lonesome after you go home by leaving lots of fingerprints all around to remind her of your visit.

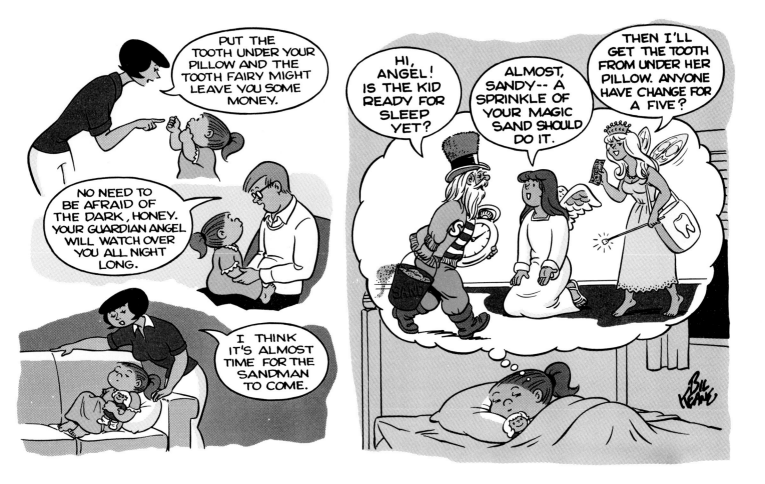

LATER

I CAN'T **FIND** MY SMILE!

A YOUNG REPORTER INTERVIEWS BIL KEANE

Q: Thank you for inviting me into your home, Mr. Keane. May I ask you a few simple questions?

A: If you don't mind simple answers. And I do mean simple!

Q: We asked Billy to name his favorite day of the year. Then we asked Dolly, Jeffy and PJ. Which is YOUR favorite?

A: I guess PJ is. He's the littlest.

Q: Which day of the year is your favorite?

A: The 29th of February. It comes around once every four years. If that was my birthday I'd only be 17. What a great age!

Q: Wasn't THE FAMILY CIRCUS born on February 29th?

A: Yes, in 1960.

Q: Probably a time you remember more than any other date.

A: No. There was this cute blonde I took to my senior prom 'way back in nineteen…nineteen hundred and…

Q: Forty?

A: No, she was only 17. What a great age!

Q: Could we move on to a different area?

A: Certainly. How about the kitchen?

Q: Do you ever run into writer's block as you go THROUGH THE YEAR WITH THE FAMILY CIRCUS?

A: Hey! That's a good title for a book!

Q: "Through the Year With the Family Circus?"

A: No, WRITER'S BLOCK! It could be a book of nothing but blank pages.

Q: Does facing the task of creating 365 new cartoons each year ever give you pause?

A: No, but Sam and Barfy often give me paws.

Q: How about Holidays? It must be difficult to attack them each year from a different angle.

A: I never attack holidays. Gets me in trouble with religious groups and patriots.

Q: What is the one thing about your job that bugs you most?

A: Giving interviews.

Q: Well, thank you, Mr. Keane, for the time.

A: It's three forty-five. By the way, how old are you?

Q: Seventeen. Go ahead, say It…

A: What a great age!